Ten Tips for Parenting
the
Smartphone Generation

GREGORY L. JANTZ, PHD
WITH ANN MCMURRAY

..., California

AspirePress

Ten Tips for Parenting the Smartphone Generation
Copyright © 2016 Gregory L. Jantz
All rights reserved.
Aspire Press, an imprint of Rose Publishing, Inc.
17909 Adria Maru Lane
Carson, CA 90746 USA
www.aspirepress.com

Register your book at www.rose-publishing.com/register
and receive a FREE *How to Study the Bible* PDF
to print for your personal or ministry use.

The views and opinions expressed in this book are those of the author(s) and do not necessarily express the views of Aspire Press, nor is this book intended to be a substitute for mental health treatment or professional counseling.

All scripture quotations, unless otherwise indicated, are taken from the Holy Bible, New International Version®, NIV®. Copyright ©1973, 1978, 1984, 2011 by Biblica, Inc.™ Used by permission of Zondervan. All rights reserved worldwide. www.zondervan.com The "NIV" and "New International Version" are trademarks registered in the United States Patent and Trademark Office by Biblica, Inc.™

Printed in the United States of America
010516RRD

Contents

Fish *and* Scorpions

There it is in its cushioned box, a technological marvel, a computer in miniature. Such a pretty pink and purple swirly case. It cost you an arm and a leg, but it's the latest phone. She squeals in delight, as she rips off the wrapping and holds it close to her preadolescent chest. Smiling from ear to ear, she runs and hugs you, saying thank-you over and over. She's thrilled and so are you, at least with the response. You're both smiling on the outside, but inside you keep pushing down that pesky twinge of doubt. You begin your mantra about why and how and when she can use it. She nods like she's hearing you, but you're not sure she is. She's not looking at you; she's looking at *it*, enthralled.

Your little girl is growing up and everyone has these things now, so what could be the harm?

■ ■ ■

After hounding you for weeks, which seems like *months* to a frazzled adult and *years* to an impatient teen, you're on your way to the electronics store to get that newest game—the one on the commercial last night with the lifelike graphics that blew you away. The TV commercial rekindled his complaints and incessant comparisons to other, cooler, parents. Admit it; he broke down your barriers. And once you're in, you're all in. Nothing halfway, even if it means you've got to upgrade the game system, too. This is going to cost you, but you plan to put to rest who the coolest parent around is, at least until the next version comes out.

He's older now; he can handle this stuff, right? How much trouble can he get into sitting in the family room with his friends?

■ ■ ■

Parental Worries

How much trouble, indeed? As parents, it's our job to worry. We worry about all sorts of things concerning our kids. In this age of technology, we get to add gadgets and gizmos and networks and devices to the list of things our parents and grandparents never had to worry about.

The Family Online Safety Institute conducted a survey about the top day-to-day concerns parents had about their children:

- 75 percent worried about their personal safety

- 67 percent worried about maintaining their privacy

- 55 percent worried about their performance in school

- 54 percent worried about their social relationships

- 51 percent worried about their physical health

- 47 percent worried about their behavior

EIGHTY-ONE PERCENT [OF PARENTS] SAID THEY EITHER WORRIED A LOT, A FAIR AMOUNT, OR SOME ABOUT TECHNOLOGY USE.

Eighty-one percent said they either worried a lot, a fair amount, or some about technology use. Nineteen percent said they didn't worry at all.[1] Maybe you're part of that 1 in 5, blissfully going through life without a care in the digital world about what technology is doing to your kids. Not me; I'm with the other 81 percent who have at least some concern about how all of this technology is going to work out.

The Internet security company ESET® did its own survey of the top Internet concerns of parents:

- 88 percent worried about what their kids could access online

- 81 percent worried about their kids visiting inappropriate websites

- 71 percent were worried about their kids giving out private information to strangers online

- 61 percent worried about their kids spending too much time with their devices

ESET's answer? They're an Internet security company, so they came up with a new parental control app. Of course, the best parental control app doesn't do any good if it's not installed on your child's devices. According to ESET's product manager, Branilav Orlik, "While we weren't completely surprised that most parents worry about what their kids' access online, we were shocked by how few had done anything about it."[2]

Fish *and* Scorpions

Do you remember the Transformers? They were children's toys from the '80s that later became a television series and then a series of movies.

Transformers were harmless vehicles, like cars and trucks, that transformed into mechanical robots. I think technology is like a transformer; it has the ability to start out as one thing and turn into something else. The question is, does technology become a good Autobot or an evil Decepticon?

We want the best for our kids. We want them to be savvy about this new technology. It drives our new economy, so we don't want them to miss out. But technology creates a tension: there is so much that's good, but we also hear about the bad. And the bad makes us worry. We wonder just what it is that we're giving our kids.

Jesus once asked an important parenting question: "Which of you fathers, if your son asks for a fish, will give him a snake instead? Or if he asks for an egg, will give him a scorpion?" (Luke 11:11–12). Jesus went on to say that even earthly parents know how to give their children good gifts. The difference between a fish and a snake, between an egg and a scorpion, is obvious.

> "IF ANY OF YOU LACKS WISDOM, YOU SHOULD ASK GOD, WHO GIVES GENEROUSLY TO ALL WITHOUT FINDING FAULT, AND IT WILL BE GIVEN TO YOU."
> —JAMES 1:5

Technology isn't always so obvious. How can we make sure our good gifts of technology (that we mean to be fish and eggs) don't turn into something else (like snakes and scorpions) that might come back to strike and sting our children?

Technology is new but wisdom is not. Parents can use wisdom to navigate the currents of this digital stream we live in. When we're short on that wisdom, we can ask God to provide it.

So take heart. Here are ten parenting tips for technology, because technology isn't going away—nor should it. As parents we just need to be smarter, wiser, and more alert than those who would seek to harm our children. That particular parental responsibility is anything but new.

TIP #1

Practice What You Preach

"I'm not going to say it again: time for dinner!" Mark could hear the frustration in his wife, Trisha's, voice. The older the kids got, the longer it seemed to take them to get to the table. After a moment, during which he vacillated between whether or not he should add his voice to Trisha's, he heard the various bedroom doors open and feet shuffling down the hall toward the kitchen. *Hmm,* he thought, *all three are here tonight.* He was never sure how many would show up for dinner.

Sam and Charlie were walking with their heads down over their phones. He could hear Kaitlyn bringing up the rear, talking on hers. Mark's frustration level zoomed up to match Trisha's. *Couldn't they go a minute without being on those annoying phones? That's all they seem to want to do.* Of course, the kids knew the rules—no cell phones at dinner—so Mark watched as they reluctantly detached from their phones, placed them on the desk, and came toward the table. All of them looked resentful and surly. *So much for engaging family conversation tonight,* he thought. *Good thing the game is on.* Mark hurried to pick up the remote and snatch the best chair to see the television.

■ ■ ■

Double Standards

Have you ever noticed that double standards don't work well with kids, especially teenagers? They have an uncanny ability to uncover them and an irritating tendency to mention them—at the most inopportune moments.

- If you, as a parent, give your teen grief over the hours spent on his or her cell phone, yet you spend at least as much time yourself watching television, you're due for a double-standard reaction.

- If you knock on your teenager's door at the wee hours of the night, tersely commanding all device use to stop, you may be asked how come you're still up doing work emails.

■ And if you're on the sidelines at the soccer game, more engrossed in the action on your phone than the action on the pitch, don't be surprised if you get pushback in the car on the way home when you complain about your teen being on his or her phone.

Double standards are confusing to young children and exasperating to teens. Confusion and exasperation are not part of God's parenting plan: "Fathers, do not exasperate your children; instead, bring them up in the training and instruction of the Lord" (Ephesians 6:4).

Proverbs puts it more plainly, "The LORD detests double standards; he is not pleased by dishonest scales" (Proverbs 20:23, NLT). You cannot have one set of rules for you and one set of rules for everyone else. Before you examine the use of technology by your children, you must first examine your own attitudes regarding the use of technology.

The Barna Group, a Christian research firm, noted:

When it comes to technology and its effects, we often approach the issue as if kids are the outlaws and as if parents are the sheriffs. . . . In fact, it is not kids who have brought the widespread use of technology into the home, it is us. They remain as impressionable as we fear they are and as we hope they are, and they model with technology what they see in the home from their parents. . . . Ultimately, we should decide what type of relationship we want our kids to have with technology and then we should do it.[3]

> Double standards are confusing to young children and exasperating to teens.
>
> "FATHERS, DO NOT EXASPERATE YOUR CHILDREN; INSTEAD, BRING THEM UP IN THE TRAINING AND INSTRUCTION OF THE LORD"
> —EPHESIANS 6:4

What sort of relationship do you want to have with technology? If you don't intentionally answer that question, your kids will likely model what you do instead of what you want.

If you are an avid technology user yourself, the questions you ask will be different from those who dislike and distrust technology. If there isn't a tech toy you can say no to, ask yourself the following questions about your own technology use. (For clarification, by "technology" I mean all of it: television, computer, tablet, cell phone, Smart phone, gaming consoles, etc. By "use" I mean use for activities from business to leisure.)

- [ ] What methods of technology do I use regularly?

- [ ] How much time do I spend with technology, including television, in the presence of my kids?

- [ ] How interactive is my technology use? Are my kids invited to participate in my use of technology?

- [ ] Have I ever appeared to choose spending time with my technology over spending time with family?

- [ ] Do I give my kids technology they can use so that I have more time to use my technology?

- [ ] Would I rather spend time with technology than spend time outside?

- [ ] Do I allow technology to interfere with my relationships?

- [ ] Do I allow technology to interfere with sleeping or eating?

- [ ] Have family members ever complained about my use of technology?

- [ ] Do I become irritable or frustrated if I cannot use my technology?

- [ ] Have I ever felt guilty about the amount of time I spend on my technology?

Do I continue my present pattern of using technology despite having witnessed or experienced negative consequences?

The last six questions are modified from the Narcotics Anonymous questionnaire "Am I an Addict?" I just substituted technology for drugs. Don't be fooled; both can be highly addictive.

What about those of you who don't really like technology? You moderately tolerate it but are suspicious and distrustful. Ask yourself the following questions:

1. What do I like about technology?

2. What do I dislike about technology?

3. Do I ever feel at a disadvantage with my child over technology?

4. What are the top three concerns I have about technology?

5. What evidence do I have for naming those top three things? Have any of those happened in my own life or the life of a member of my family?

6. What am I afraid will happen if I say yes to technology?

Your relationship with technology—or lack thereof—will affect your relationship with your kids, who are growing up in a culture where technology is a part of daily life and experiences. When you approach a component of their lives with such suspicion, you may create a wedge between yourself and your children. If you exaggerate the dangers technology poses to your children specifically and to life generally, you may degrade your credibility on other, more important topics. If you alienate yourself from your children over technology, you may leave the door open for others to enter into their sphere of influence.

YOUR RELATIONSHIP WITH TECHNOLOGY—OR LACK THEREOF—WILL AFFECT YOUR RELATIONSHIP WITH YOUR KIDS.

Where technology is concerned, I've seen people from two extremes: absolute adoration or absolute suspicion. Most people, however, fall somewhere in the middle, and each of us needs to determine where we fall on that spectrum. I confess to being more toward the adoration side. I didn't realize how much that attitude was affecting my children until confronted one day, when I appeared on local television.

Public Display

One of our local television stations runs a morning show in which I occasionally participate. Usually I speak about mental health issues or how people are affected by local or national events. On this particular morning, I was asked to speak about the effects of technology. I brought along a basket full of family devices to use as examples. My two boys, who didn't happen to have school that day, wanted to come along, so I brought them with me to the station. I thought it would be fun for them to watch Dad live on TV.

To get ready, I displayed on the set's coffee table all of the devices I'd brought. The technology segment started, and the host quickly commented on how many

I'd brought. When I put them out, I'd been happy how many there were, but now her comment made me think. I had to admit in front of thousands of viewers that, well, there were probably more gadgets than my kids really needed.

Before I knew it, my boys were invited onto the set to participate in the discussion about our family's use of technology! As I watched my boys talk about the technology displayed in front of them—technology that, mostly, I had bought for them—I had to admit my own adoration for technology was definitely influencing theirs.

After that segment was over, I rounded up my boys and all of our technology and went home. A part of me was tempted to start weeding out the sheer number of devices, but I didn't. I recognized that doing so would create a double standard because I wasn't, honestly, ready to do the same with my own devices—not yet, anyway. Instead, I went home and sat down with my wife and discussed how our (my) ties to technology had gotten a bit out of control. I recognized I couldn't demand of my boys what I wasn't first willing to do for myself.

My epiphany had come in front of a whole lot of people. Yours needn't be as dramatic. But I encourage you to confront your relationship with technology, nonetheless. In some ways, I had turned technology into a sort of idol. I was using technology to direct my life (and my work), to solve my problems, to distract me from difficulty, to provide entertainment and comfort. That was far too much power to give inanimate objects.

I was putting too much faith in my technology. Before I worked with my sons, I needed to confront whether I'd slipped into the do-as-I-say-not-as-I-do trap found in Romans: "You, then, who teach others, do you not teach yourself? You who preach against stealing, do you steal yourself?" (Romans 2:21).

Test yourself where it comes to technology. Know how you relate to it and how you want your children to relate to it. Once you understand where you want the relationship to go, you can start to create thoughtful reasons for the limits and rules you place around technology—limits and rules you can both explain to your children and keep yourself. What you say must match what you do. Speech and action—both are vital to avoid double standards. We are the technology template our children duplicate.

TIP #2

Figure Out How Much Is Too Much

Last year, I ran across an Amazon ad for the Fisher-Price IPad Apptivity Seat. This infant seat had an "option to insert iPad (not included) into the mirror's case."[4] My initial reaction was *You've got to be kidding! An iPad for an infant?*

I flashed to the scene in the Disney movie *Wall-E* where the pudgy, flabby humans aboard the spaceship move themselves around on glorified bouncy seats and have conversations via screens with people right next to them, instead of simply turning their heads to talk. If you've never seen this movie, I encourage you to do so. Like many children's movies, the themes speak straight to the hearts of adults. Or you can go to YouTube and search for "Human Dystopia."[5] I think you'll find that the resemblance to the IPad Apptivity Seat is nothing short of eerie.

Apparently, my shocked response was not uncommon. There was a flurry of negative comments on Amazon, including one person who said that with more enhancements, parents wouldn't even have to touch their children. Negative articles began to pop up in the news as well. I'm not sure when Fisher-Price pulled the plug on this baby bouncy seat, but pull the plug they did, marking it "Discontinued by Manufacturer" with a handful still left to be purchased.

■ ■ ■

Excessive Media Use

The American Academy of Pediatrics (AAP) recommends no screen time for children under two and a maximum of one to two hours of entertainment screen time per day for other children. In their statement, the AAP said:

> Excessive media use has been associated with obesity, lack of sleep, school problems, aggression and other behavior issues. A recent study shows that the average 8- to 10-year-old spends nearly 8 hours a day with different media, and older

children and teens spend more than 11 hours per day. Kids who have a TV in their bedroom spend more time with media. About 75 percent of 12- to 17-year-olds own cell phones, and nearly all teenagers use text messaging.[6]

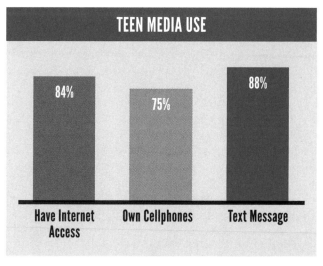

"Children, Adolescents, and the Media," Pediatrics (November 2013), http://pediatrics.aappublications.org/content/132/5/958

So how are parents doing with limiting screen time, especially for younger children? A WebMD article reports that "nearly all U.S. kids under age 4 have used a mobile device such as a tablet or smartphone, and they are using them at earlier and earlier ages, a new study finds."[7] The results prompted concern from healthcare professionals: Dr. Danelle Fisher is quoted as saying, "Parents in this study admitted to using mobile media for their children to keep them quiet or entertained in public places or in place of the interaction at bedtime. . . . Children need parental interaction for many reasons and this trend is, overall, worrisome."[8]

Screen Time *vs.* Face Time

How much time do your children spend in front of a screen each day? Have you ever added it up?

Using the table on pages 26-27, tally up, on average, the hours each day that your children spend interacting with a screen. Compute separate totals for each child.

Once you've done that, add the total for each column to get the total time for *all* screens each day.

Multiply that total to see how much screen time each child is getting every week; then calculate the total for every month. And if you really want a wake-up call, figure out how many *days* of screen time is each child getting in a year.

As a parent, consider the following questions:

- How are you doing at spending time interacting with your children, no matter their age?

- How do the hours your children spend interacting with a screen compare to the time spent interacting with you—in both quantity and quality?

A later chapter, "Tip #4: Find the Off Switch," will help you determine limits for technology use for your family. But it's up to you to determine the amount of time you spend interacting directly with your children.

	Televisions/ DVDs	Computers/ Laptops/ Tablets	Video Game Systems
Home			
School			
Daycare/ Childcare			
Homes of Friends			
Other			
TOTAL of each type			

Automotive Entertainment System	Phone	Other	TOTAL at each location

AAP Recommendations

The AAP has put out a statement about how parents should interact with media, or what we've been referring to as technology. Read the list of suggestions below from the AAP, and determine when you are going to implement each one. Number each item in the order you want to incorporate them into your family routine. Consider a multiphase plan that over time will allow you to implement all of the suggestions.

> Being on top of technology today is only prudent.
>
> "A PRUDENT PERSON FORESEES DANGER AND TAKES PRECAUTIONS. THE SIMPLETON GOES BLINDLY ON AND SUFFERS THE CONSEQUENCES."
> —PROVERBS 22:3, NLT

■ Help children make healthy choices in their "media diet." Look at age-appropriate ratings for shows, movies, and games; and make sure children avoid seeing violent, sexually explicit content, or tobacco or alcohol glorification.

■ Teach children "media literacy" by watching television with the children, discussing and learning from the content.

- Encourage the use of nonelectronic media and formats such as books, magazines, newspapers, and board games.

- Watch children for adverse effects of excessive media consumption, such as sleep disorders, eating disorders, obesity, attention problems, and school difficulties.

- Limit media to educational content.

- Establish screen-free zones at home, including in all bedrooms.

- Turn off the television at dinnertime.

- Limit to only one or two hours per day the entertainment screen time of all children above two years of age.

- Encourage children to spend time outdoors, read, engage in hobbies, and use their imaginations during free play.[9]

Technology requires monitoring by parents. The latest-and-greatest may not be what is best for our kids. As parents, we must evaluate not only each individual piece of technology but also the cumulative effect of technology. Being on top of technology today is only prudent.

Remember—
If You Bought It, It's Yours

"*We* talked about this," Beth said, taking a deep breath.

Madison just stood in her bedroom doorway, incredulous. "But . . . but . . . you can't take away my phone!" she stated, as if this truth should be obvious.

"It's not your phone, Madison," Beth replied, trying to remain calm. "I bought that phone for you. You didn't live up to our agreement, so I'm taking your phone until your grades improve."

"But you can't take away my phone!" Madison repeated, her voice escalating as the tears threatened. "I've *got* to have it!"

"What you need to have," Beth countered, "are better grades. We talked about this a month ago. I've been watching your progress and there isn't much. You're spending too much time on your phone and not enough time on your schoolwork."

Madison immediately switched into negotiation mode. "I'll do better. I promise!"

"You *are* going to do better," Beth assured her, "and to help you do better, I'll be taking your phone for the next two weeks." Beth put out her right hand, palm up.

"What if I don't give it to you?" Madison snapped back.

Beth, ready for this, replied, "Then I'll just have to turn off the service."

"What if I sign up with another company?" Clearly, Madison had thought about this.

"You're fourteen years old, Madison. No company is going to sign you up. Just give me the phone." *Please, just give me the phone!* Beth thought to herself, though she presented no outward distress to Madison. Reluctantly, wailing that Beth was being so unfair, Madison reached into her pocket and turned over the phone.

"We'll evaluate in two weeks and see how you're doing," Beth promised, as Madison turned her back and stomped into her room.

It was going to be a long two weeks.

■ ■ ■

Strong Attraction

The scenario described above doesn't just play out for girls. Try taking a video game system away from a fourteen-year-old boy (and forbidding him to play at a friend's house—you have to be multiple steps ahead). Kids, teens especially, develop a strong attachment to their technology.

Do you remember when I took my sons to the television studio? I was challenged by the show's host about the amount of tech I'd purchased for my kids. I was also challenged by how attached, how proprietary, my sons were to "their" gadgets during that segment. I had bought those things for them, but once the technology was out of the box, I got shoved over to the side, along with the discarded wrappings.

IF YOU WANT TO KNOW IF ONE OF YOUR CHILDREN HAS BECOME ATTACHED TO A PIECE OF TECHNOLOGY, TRY TAKING THAT TECHNOLOGY AWAY.

Do you ever feel shoved aside as soon as the box containing some piece of tech you've bought is opened? The device becomes primary and you become secondary. The device now belongs to them. Besides, they're not even sure you know how to use it! It's a running joke that if an adult has a problem with a piece of technology, he or she just needs to ask the nearest eight-year-old.

Kids are comfortable around technology. Have you ever seen one of them read an instruction manual with a new device or game? Instead, they use the device to learn how to use the device. They talk with their friends and share tips and tricks. If they get stuck, they go to

YouTube to find a fix. They spend time getting to know the device, pushing buttons and clicking options, just to see where each takes them. They're fearless. Why shouldn't they be? They didn't buy it!

I found in my own household that mastery over a device equates in young minds to ownership. In their minds, the true owner of the device is not the person who bought it; the true owner of the device is the person who knows best how to use it. This is a subtle distinction but one that I've found is prevalent with kids and technology. If you want to know if one of your children has become attached to a piece of technology, try taking that technology away.

| Youthful Appendage

A couple of years ago, I ran across a fascinating article that illustrated the bond that technology can create in those who use it. The article described how people jokingly refer to technology as an appendage to young people, but that the joke may not be so funny. When asked, over half the teens and young adults polled said they would sooner give up their sense of smell than their technology. Though older generations may view technology as an enrichment, our children see it as essential. They use it as a way to "sense the world and make sense of the world."[10]

What struck me most about this article was the idea that this generation considers technology like an appendage. The device you buy becomes, in their minds, as connected to them as an arm or a leg. Ask them to cut it off and the reaction can be significant. Over half of them would call your bluff and give up their sense of smell, before they'd let you pry their fingers off their tech.

Again, the point is that the way *you* view the technology in your home may be vastly different from the way *your children* do. What is the answer, then? Just give in to the childish outburst or teenage tantrum? No, the answer is to prepare yourself to be a parent, even when you face stubborn children.

Your children may view that cell phone or game console or tablet or whatever-comes-next like a part of themselves, but you are still the parent. Even if you didn't buy the device, that device is in your home and under your authority. You may not understand how to use it, but your children still need to obey you where that device is concerned. This Biblical admonition may have been written millennia ago, but it is still in effect today: "Children, obey your parents in everything, for this pleases the Lord" (Colossians 3:20).

Some parents may be tempted to give technology to their children for the wrong reasons:

- to entertain them or keep them busy while the parent is doing something else;

- to demonstrate how cool they are in an attempt to be buddy instead of parent;

- as a way to assuage guilt over being gone or being unavailable due to commitments or situations such as work or divorce.

Technology should not be used as a babysitter, as a banner, or as a bribe. Children can be tempted to use technology the wrong way, but parents can also be tempted to give technology for the wrong reasons.

Even if your motives were not completely pure when you brought technology into the home, you can still begin to reframe it under parental authority. Whatever your situation, don't back down where technology is concerned. We live in a new digital landscape, but you are still expected to be the parent. Our kids may be identified as the new global generation or as digital natives, but they are still our kids.

> Even if you didn't buy the device, that device is in your home and under your authority.

As you enter into the battlefield for the hearts and minds of your children, consider the encouragement the Lord gave Joshua and take heart as a parent: "Be strong and courageous. Do not be afraid or terrified because of them, for the Lord your God goes with you; he will never leave you nor forsake you" (Deuteronomy 31:6).

TIP #4

Find the Off Switch

"Ahhhhhh!" Ted screamed, louder than he meant to.

Jacob barely glanced up from his game to ask, "What's wrong, Dad?"

Though he hated to admit it, Ted said, "I'm just not getting these alerts on my phone. I've tried the vibration, the ringing, the beeping, but every time I look at my phone, I've missed something!" Ted was loath to admit he wasn't feeling the vibration because he often forgot his phone and left it lying around. He hated to confess to Jacob that it was getting harder and harder to hear the buzzes and beeps and squawks he'd set up.

"Set up a flash," Jacob suggested, eyes centered on his game, his thumbs flying over the controller.

"How do I do that?" Ted asked.

Jacob rattled off a series of instructions in rapid fire, never once looking up from his game. "And what will that do?" Ted asked, exasperated, lost in the process.

Scoring, Jacob turned and looked over his shoulder, confused as to why Ted wasn't following the conversation. "It'll make your phone flash when you get an alert, like a text or call coming in. That's what you wanted, right?"

"Huh . . . thanks," Ted replied, walking out and letting Jacob get back to his game. *How does he come up with this stuff?* Ted wondered, feeling a little older and a little dumber, which wasn't a good combination for him.

■ ■ ■

Parental Control

As adults, some of us have to admit we're not going to know more about these devices than our kids. Other adults just aren't interested. Those of us who are interested find we don't have the time it takes to figure out all the features and functions. Our time is taken up making the money to buy the devices in the first place. Kids, however, have the time to figure this stuff out. They also have friends to figure out what they haven't.

Not knowing more than your kids would seem counterproductive for parental authority. However, a full working knowledge of any device is not needed to exercise parental control. You don't need to know how each thing works; you just need to know how to turn the darn thing off. Technically, you don't even have to know where the off switch is, as long as your kids do and you're in control of your kids.

Just because a device has an on switch doesn't mean it has to be on all the time. This concept, however, can be counterintuitive to kids who grew up with the television on anytime someone was home—not even in the room, just home. Or to kids who grew up riding around in a car that always had the radio on, switching from station to station to find something—anything—to listen to instead of, say, carrying on a conversation or just watching the scenery in silence. As adults, we have established some of the ground rules for this new technology by the way we've dealt with the old technology. We are reaping what we've sown.

A FULL WORKING KNOWLEDGE OF ANY DEVICE IS NOT NEEDED TO EXERCISE PARENTAL CONTROL.

Reasonable Limits

When limits for technology are being defined, all members of the family need to be considered. One person may buy the technology, but another person uses it. The person who uses the technology does so in relationship with others. However, as the parent, you remain the authority in the family—yours is the final decision. You want to guide your family in how to best integrate technology, including creating reasonable limits.

■ INITIATE A FAMILY DISCUSSION ABOUT TECHNOLOGY.

Sometimes as adults, we discover an issue in our family we want to change. So we read about it, think about it, and come to our own conclusions about what we should do. Then we move to implement those conclusions.

> As adults, we have established some of the ground rules for this new technology by the way we've dealt with the old technology. We are reaping what we've sown.
>
> "DO NOT BE DECEIVED: GOD CANNOT BE MOCKED. A MAN REAPS WHAT HE SOWS."
> —GALATIANS 6:7

The difficulty with this approach is all of the groundwork has been confined to us. We only bring others into the process at the very end, at the change part. Not having gone through the full process, others may not be at the same place and may resent being asked or required to change abruptly. This is not unlike the parent concerned about weight gain, who suddenly announces to the family that there will be no more cookies in the house. Rarely does this sort of heavy-handed announcement go over well.

> Avoid dominating a family discussion about technology.
>
> "MY DEAR BROTHERS AND SISTERS, TAKE NOTE OF THIS: EVERYONE SHOULD BE QUICK TO LISTEN, SLOW TO SPEAK AND SLOW TO BECOME ANGRY."
> —JAMES 1:19

Here are tips for the family discussion:

- Let the family in on your concerns about how technology is affecting the family.

- Be sure to present a balanced view of technology—the positives as well as the negatives. If you tend to be suspicious and distrust technology, be sure to confine that negativity to the device and not the person using it.

- Be willing to open up the dialogue and listen to both sides of the equation—including how *your* technology use and attitude affect others.

- Avoid dominating the discussion. How you frame the conversation can have tremendous impact over its outcome.

■ START SMALL WHENEVER POSSIBLE.

If someone's technology use is completely out of hand, you may need to take accelerated action. Generally, though, the best way to get results is slowly, over time. Think of the tortoise and the hare; being slow and steady wins the race. Instead of decreeing that your children go from using technology for six hours a day to a single hour, try cutting the time in half. You can also discuss what the kids would think would be a reasonable amount of time and seek to come to an initial compromise. Be prepared to cut down your own use of technology, as a show of good faith and a willingness to model change.

■ REPLACE INSTEAD OF REDUCE OR REMOVE.

Whenever possible, work with each member of the family to come up with positive replacements for technology use. For example, replace tech time with:

- **Homework**—Offer to provide a comfortable family space and include parental assistance.

- **Outside activity**—Offer to go to a local park together or assist with signing up for a sports team. Go for a family walk.

- **Family activities**—Enjoy game nights, sit-down dinners, or movie nights.

■ BE CLEAR ON THE LIMITS AND STICK TO THEM.

If you are the main person driving these limits, you will come under increased scrutiny

> Be prepared to cut down your own use of technology, as a show of good faith and a willingness to model change.
>
> "WE DID THIS, NOT BECAUSE WE DO NOT HAVE THE RIGHT TO SUCH HELP, BUT IN ORDER TO OFFER OURSELVES AS A MODEL FOR YOU TO IMITATE."
> —2 THESSALONIANS 3:9

to make sure you're following your own rules. You'll also be pushed to see just how serious you are about maintaining the limits. A word of caution here—limits are difficult to maintain unless *all* the adults in the extended family adhere to the rules as well. You may need to work privately with some family members to gain their buy-in.

> As a leader in your family, you need to make sure that your yes is always yes and your no is always no; in other words, be consistent.

The best thing to do is to have the limits clearly understood by everyone in the family. You could even write the rules down and post them in a central location. As a leader in your family, you need to make sure that your yes is always yes and your no is always no; in other words, be consistent.

▪ DETERMINE THE CONSEQUENCES AHEAD OF TIME.

That the limits will be challenged is not a question of if, but of when. So at the time you discuss the tech limits, you need to close the loop and determine what the consequences will be if the limits aren't honored.

- Allow family members to have input about the consequences for violating the limits. People seem to accept consequences more easily if they've had a part in determining them.

- Be sure to keep the consequence in line with the offense.

In other words, allow the punishment to fit the crime, and allow family members to help you determine what that punishment will be. If you don't, you run the risk of alienating your family.

■ ALLOW FOR FLEXIBILITY.

If your son or daughter gets a last-minute invitation to a friend's house to participate in a multi-player gaming event and he or she has already used up gaming time that week, be flexible. If you know and approve of the friend, you can make an exception for that occasion. The limits are there to protect family values and provide structure. When rules become rules for rules' sake, they lose

> As the parental authority in your family, you want to be a servant leader, not a tyrant.

their power, and people are more willing to break them. These limits are there to serve your family, not set you up as Technology Overlord.

As the parental authority in your family, you want to be a servant leader, not a tyrant. Your motivation for the limits you help to initiate is to serve your family, not unduly frustrate them. Help them to understand your point of view, seek to understand theirs, and together work toward keeping technology as a positive in your family.

Watch Out for the Bad

First, there was a general listlessness, a residual sadness in his demeanor that alerted Cindy something was wrong. But it can be impossible to get a fifteen-year-old boy to tell you anything. Then, there were the excuses to not go to school. But what kid really wants to go to school, especially as the year winds down? She kept asking if something was wrong, but all she got were vague responses. Tyler spent a lot of time in his room, which wasn't unusual, but there weren't any sounds of him playing video games. When she'd knock on his door and go in, he'd be sitting on his bed.

Two weeks came and went and things weren't getting better. That's when Julie called. She'd heard from her son, a friend of Tyler's, that Tyler was being mocked at school. Apparently, Tyler had developed on Facebook a relationship with a girl at school. What Tyler didn't know was, the girl was conducting those online conversations in the presence of a group of her friends, who would laugh and ridicule Tyler and compose just the right type of responses to get Tyler to reveal more and more about himself.

This went on for several weeks, with this "reality show" being played out at school. Tyler was thrilled to finally be getting a girlfriend. The girl and her friends were thrilled over this novel form of entertainment. Of course, they couldn't keep such a good thing to themselves. It wasn't long before the group of people who knew about the budding "relationship" expanded.

Julie's son, Cameron, found out about it and told Tyler. What good friend wouldn't? By that time, though, the damage had already been done to Tyler's fragile, fifteen-year-old self-esteem.

Cameron told his mother what was going on with Tyler when Julie had commented on a cyber-bullying story she saw on the Internet. Cameron calmly said that happened all the time and mentioned Tyler. Julie wasn't sure Cindy knew and decided to call her just to be sure.

When she got off the phone with Julie, Cindy felt sick. The teenage years were bad enough without stuff like this happening. Tyler had opened up to this girl and now his words were making the rounds at school. No wonder he didn't want to go. Cindy was sure that many of the kids wouldn't participate in the gossip and ridicule, but there only had to be a few who did to make Tyler's life difficult. The question was, how could she possibly make it better?

■ ■ ■

Two Categories *of* Danger

The first category of danger involving technology deals with content. The second category of danger deals with use. In both cases, the degree of the danger involved may differ from slight to very serious. And the consequences can vary also. This is why monitoring the use of technology (discussed in detail in "Tip #8: Find Out What You Don't Know") is so very important.

Content

The first category of danger involving technology is associated with the content. For example, there are negatives associated with accessing violent or sexually explicit material. In this case, the content creates negative consequences.

There are filtering program and apps designed to significantly reduce a child's access to violent or sexually explicit material. Are these 100 percent foolproof? No, nothing is; but these products can go a long way toward parental peace of mind. Internet filters—from fee-based to free—block access to IP addresses, filter inappropriate content, manage usage, and monitor activities. Which product is best for your family depends upon your situation. I typed in "top parent internet filters" into my browser and got multiple websites, from third-party review sites to product websites. If finances are an issue, type in "top free parental internet filters."

Content on the Internet can be generated by products and websites. Content can also be generated by individual people. Tyler wasn't connecting with the wrong website; Tyler was connecting with the wrong person. Sadly, no amount of filtering can keep one person from harassing or bullying another. The content of a text or a post can be just as damaging as an inappropriate website. In some cases, the content is more damaging because it is personally directed.

The sheer creativity of technology has opened up a Pandora's box of unexpected parenting challenges. In my day, my parents might have worried about me getting a hold of a *Playboy*. Now, I worry about my teenage boys being sexted by another teenager.

My parents could control what I saw and heard when I was at home, because they controlled the switches to the television and to the radio, and they had the key to the front door. They controlled the access points into our family. Technology has created multiple access points for our kids, and we are the ones who have purchased those connections.

> Build a strong foundation with your children so that when something negative happens, they can come to you.
>
> "WHOEVER CONCEALS THEIR SINS DOES NOT PROSPER, BUT THE ONE WHO CONFESSES AND RENOUNCES THEM FINDS MERCY."
> —PROVERBS 28:13

Tyler wasn't harmed by surfing anarchist or pornographic websites. He was harmed by his conversing online with a girl at school. If it hadn't been on Facebook, it could have been by text messages. The best defense parents have is solid relationships with their children. Control what you can, but realize you can't control everything. Instead, build a strong foundation with your children so that when something negative happens, they can come to you.

■ ■ ■

Cindy knocked on the door and said, "Can we talk?" The door opened and Tyler warily said, "What about?"

"I know what's going on at school with that girl," she said simply. She could tell Tyler was taken aback; but instead of saying something, he just went to sit on his bed, so she followed him into the room, choosing to sit on his desk chair.

"How did you find out?" he asked.

"That doesn't matter right now," Cindy said. "Right now, what matters is *you*." Over the next twenty minutes, she was able to get Tyler to open up, a little, about how he was feeling. His shame and humiliation cut through her like a knife; but she kept her feelings in check, so she could concentrate on what Tyler needed. They'd get through this, but Tyler's pain wouldn't be fading anytime soon.

■ ■ ■

Use

The second category of danger involving technology is associated with use. I suppose it's not a coincidence that people talk about *using* drugs and *using* technology. Both are powerful stimulants that affect the mind and body. And there can be unpleasant consequences to the use of both as well.

Physical Effects

■ WEIGHT GAIN AND MUSCLE WEAKNESS

I suppose the most obvious danger to the physical body due to the use—or overuse—of technology results because so much of technology is done while staying relatively still. This lack of activity can lead to obesity and muscle weakness. And let's not forget about the snacking that often also goes hand-in-hand with gaming!

■ INSUFFICIENT SLEEP

I have teenagers and I find it increasingly difficult to get them to go to bed on time. With the demands of school and extracurricular activities, lights-out at the Jantz household can creep into the late hours of the night. Add the effects of technology on a busy household, and sleep patterns are sure to be disrupted. According to the National Sleep Foundation, the average teenager needs eight to ten hours of sleep per night.[11] How about your kids? Are they routinely getting enough sleep?

THE MAJORITY OF TEENS—OVER 70 PERCENT—HAVE AT LEAST TWO ELECTRONIC DEVICES IN THEIR BEDROOMS AT NIGHT.

According to a study by the Australian Broadcasting Association, "Use of computers, cell phones and televisions at higher doses was associated with delayed sleep/wake schedules and wake lag, potentially impairing health and educational outcomes."[12] The study also found that the majority of teens—over 70 percent—have at least two electronic devices in their bedrooms at night.

Where sleep and tech are concerned, the National Sleep Foundation recommends some solutions:

- **Make sleep a priority.**

  I agree! Healthy sleep is as important as healthy eating and healthy physical activity. Sleep must take priority over tech.

- **Make the bedroom a sleep haven.**

  This means no television or game console. While your teen is powering up with sleep, their devices (laptops, cell phones, tablets) can be powering up in a common area.

- **Establish a sleep/wake routine and stick to it, even on the weekends.**

  I realize staying up until two in the morning with television or tech is a time-honored adolescent tradition; but for the health of your teen, the only honoring that needs to happen is towards sleep.

- **Avoid technology and media consumption an hour before going to sleep.**

  The body and brain need some offline downtime to prepare for sleep.[13]

■ TEXT NECK AND TEXT THUMB

"We did a study on the issue of poor posture and how it affects you, especially when you're on a cell phone or smart device. . . . It's a lot of load, an amazing amount of weight to be carrying around your neck." So says Kenneth K. Hansraj, MD.[14] Tech neck is a repetitive stress injury due to how we physically hunker over our phones.

Not to be outdone, there is now also text thumb. According to an article on ergonomics, text thumb is "a repetitive stress injury that affects the thumb and wrist. Pain and sometimes a popping sound are present on the outside of the thumb at or near the wrist. There can also be a decrease in grip strength or range of motion."[15]

How do you cut down on the possibility of repetitive stress injuries? Don't engage in the activity as much or as often. Take breaks to move around, stretch, bend, and use those muscles and tendons in different ways.

■ EYE AND EAR STRAIN

I spend a great deal of time looking at screens and by the end of the day, my eyes sometimes ache. Technology can have the same effect on children, especially after long periods of screen time. In addition, earbuds cranked up for maximum effect can, over time, cause maximum damage to fragile eardrums.

Social-Emotional Effects

■ CONTINUOUS PARTIAL ATTENTION

The concept of continuous partial attention was articulated by Linda Stone: "To pay continuous partial attention is to pay partial attention— *continuously.*"[16] This sounds like multitasking, but

Stone notes a significant difference. In multitasking, the goal is to do as many things as possible to increase productivity. But with continuous partial attention, the goal is not productivity but connectivity. Children, teens especially, have a desire to belong, to connect with their peer group and with technology. Now they can, 24/7.

WHEN KIDS CONTINUOUSLY DEVOTE PARTIAL ATTENTION TO THEIR TECH, THEY ARE DEVOTING PARTIAL ATTENTION TO EVERYTHING ELSE.

How can staying connected to friends be a bad thing? Kids have always been connected to friends. The difference that technology makes is the immediacy and the urgency that immediacy produces. Stone goes on to explain, "It is an always-on, anywhere, anytime, any place behavior that involves an artificial sense of constant crisis."[17] When kids continuously devote partial attention to their tech, they are, by definition, devoting partial attention to everything else.

■ ACQUIRED ATTENTION DEFICIT DISORDER (ADD)

If a person is in continuous partial attention, isn't that person also in continuous partial *distraction*? This tech-driven state of partial attention/ partial distraction may create distractibility as compelling as ADD. This is the theory of Dr. John Ratey: "Several years ago, Dr. John Ratey, a clinical associate profession of psychiatry at Harvard [and author of *Delivered from Distractions*], began using the term 'acquired attention deficit disorder' to describe the condition of people who are accustomed to a constant stream of digital stimulation and feel bored in the absence of it.[18].

■ DISCONNECT ANXIETY

Have you ever noticed how irritable your children become when the Internet goes out? The effect can be nothing short of apocalyptic. Disconnect anxiety is a phrase that started popping up several years ago to explain the effects of suddenly becoming offline, with the effects ranging from mild to severe, depending upon how heavy the user. As you work toward creating limits and boundaries on the use of technology within your family, you may see instances of disconnect anxiety that range from irritability to anxiousness.

■ AGGRESSION

A recent study by the American Psychological Association concluded that "the link between violence in video games and increased aggression in players is one of the most studied and best established in the field. . . . No single risk factor consistently leads a person to act aggressively or violently. . . .Rather, it is the accumulation of risk factors that tends to lead to aggressive or violent behavior. The research reviewed here demonstrates that violent video game use is one such risk factor."[19] This doesn't mean that if your children play games that contain violence, they will grow up to be violent criminals. It does mean that playing violent games can desensitize people

Ratings by the Entertainment Software Rating Board

to violence and encourage more aggressive behavior in real life as well as while playing games.

I have a feeling this debate, which started with watching violent content on television and has moved to playing video games that have violent content, is far from over. For parents caught in the middle, the best advice I can give is to follow the recommended age ratings on games and observe your child's behavior both while playing games and in general. If you see a change in behavior, especially an increase in aggression, then you may want to review and reconsider the games your child is playing.

■ VIRTUAL REALITY

I have a concern about how kids are learning to interpret the world based on their interactions with technology. I say this because I see certain patterns developing in myself:

- I confess to increasing impatience. I expect responses, answers, and solutions immediately because, generally, technology provides them.

- I confess to decreased tolerance of complexity. I thought Dr. Elias Aboujaoude, director of Stanford University's Impulse Control

Disorders Clinic, put the challenge well: "If our attention span constricts to the point where we can only take information in 140-character sentences, then that doesn't bode too well for our future."[20]

- I confess to distractibility. With so many bits of information to look at and consider, I can be like someone at an all-you-can-eat buffet, grazing bits from appetizer to entrée to dessert without ever really stopping to eat a full meal. Nicholas Carr, in his book, *The Shallows,* highlights his concern that the quick and easily accessible flood of information is enticing us into the digital "shallows," and we're losing our capacity to concentrate and dive deep into issues and concepts.[21]

None of these perceptions represent the way the real world works.

■ FALSE INTIMACY

There is an aspect of anonymity to the Internet that doesn't make sense. On one hand, the Internet is the most public forum available. Whatever you put out there never goes away. Instead, it lingers forever, somewhere on some distant server. Yet people treat the Internet, especially social media, as if it's their own private platform. They will converse with people they would never say a word to in real life. They will divulge personal details to total strangers. The normal cautions that would kick in with face-to-face communication don't seem to apply.

THE NORMAL CAUTIONS THAT WOULD KICK IN WITH FACE-TO-FACE COMMUNICATION DON'T SEEM TO APPLY.

Children and teens can be especially vulnerable to this kind of false intimacy. We read the consequences in the news: children, especially teens, share personal secrets with one person online, only to have those secrets posted and reposted, tweeted and retweeted. Then there are the kids who send one person an intimate photo, only to have that photo show up for the perusal of strangers or sent to family out of spite and vengeance. Children don't always appreciate the long reach of the Internet, because they tend to engage in activities with a small group of peers or friends.

Facebook, especially, has redefined the term *friend* into anyone who has access to your information. Because the number of such friends has become a badge of honor, children can, sadly, allow access to people who wish to cause them harm. As the number of news stories about the dangers of too much shared information increases, I hope that all children will catch up to the danger and pay more attention to the rules parents set up about who to connect with, why, and what to put out there.

Silver Linings

Pendulums tend to swing both ways. We are currently in the midst of the onslaught of technological marvels without the benefit of hindsight. What we've come to know as the Internet (originally called the World Wide Web) is about twenty-five years old. Mobile phones have been around since the mid '70s (anyone remember the huge boxes people used to put up to their ears?) and smartphones are around twenty years old. In the grand scheme of life, none of those has been with us very long.

All of us—adults, parents, teens, and children—are in the midst of a learning curve on how to handle the changes we're experiencing. And not only parents can become weary with the downside of this digital age. Some kids are finding the shiny patina of technology wearing off a bit. According to a study by Common Sense Media, almost half the teens surveyed indicated they get frustrated with friends who choose to text or check their social media accounts when they are hanging out together. Twenty-one percent indicated that their parents spend too much time on technology.[22]

Kids are growing tired of the pressure to keep up with the constant flow of information. One 16-year-old said, "As a teen, life can be hell. Sometimes it's nice to just sit back and relax with no way possible to communicate with anyone in any way. That's why I occasionally 'lose' my cell phone."[23]

There is a definite downside to technology. But isn't there a downside to just about everything? The answer in regard to the use of technology is to treat it carefully, understanding the power it has over you and your family. This world is full of addictive behaviors, and technology is just the latest one. I don't believe

TREAT TECHNOLOGY CAREFULLY, UNDERSTANDING THE POWER IT HAS OVER YOU AND YOUR FAMILY.

the answer is to attempt to rigidly control technology, which changes almost daily. Instead, I believe the answer is to teach your children to control themselves, to be like Paul, who said: "'All things are lawful for me,' but not all things are helpful. 'All things are lawful for me,' but I will not be dominated by anything" (1 Corinthians 6:12, ESV).

Enjoy the Good

"*Come* on, Dad! I've got it set up," Eric yelled. Mark took a deep breath and put his computer to sleep. Normally, this would be the time for the two of them to go outside and play catch or soccer. But since it was 37 degrees and raining, neither of those outdoor activities was an option. This winter, they'd gotten into a routine of playing football or rock-band games together. Mark had put his foot down about a game Eric wanted that was rated 18+ and had "extensive blood and gore," violence, and profanity, though he was seriously considering a different, more age-appropriate game for Christmas.

Mark had to admit that Eric took to these games like a fish to water. Even though Mark played in a garage band right after high school, Eric wiped the floor with him in the rock-band game. They were more evenly matched playing video football, but even there Eric had the edge. Ever since Eric was able to talk his teacher into allowing football as a research project, he'd spent copious amounts of time and energy tracking the players, teams, trades, injuries—the whole nine yards. *Well,* Mark thought to himself, *he could always make a fortune someday playing fantasy football.*

Walking into the family room, Eric was just as hyped up as Mark expected, excitedly shoving the controller in Mark's direction. *Defeat is good for the soul,* Mark reminded himself, especially where his son was concerned. But as soon as the weather shifted, Eric better watch out. Mark hadn't played soccer in college for nothing!

■ ■ ■

The Snake-*and*-Dove Approach

After reading over the potential downsides to technology, some of you may be seriously reconsidering the whole thing. But before you turn your home into a Luddite colony,[24] consider this statement: "Children's experiences with technology and interactive media are increasingly part of the context of their lives, which must be considered as part of the developmentally appropriate framework."[25] Technology is now part of the social and developmental fabric of our society. As a parent, you can certainly make a decision not to have a television in your home, but your kids' friends most probably have one. You can hold off getting your ten-year-old a cell phone, but chances are, he or she is around them at or after school. You can take your kids to the library and buy all sorts of books, but even at the library, there is computer access.

Some of you are still irrepressible Pollyannas where technology is concerned and, therefore, you reject such concerns. Whenever you read about a negative, you assure yourself that it won't happen with your kids or your tech. You tell yourself, *How could something so fun and exciting and amazing possibly go wrong?*

Neither attitude, I believe, is realistic. Both openness and wariness is warranted with technology. I believe parents need to adopt the snake-and-dove approach described by Jesus: "I am sending you out like sheep among wolves. Therefore be as shrewd as snakes and as innocent as doves" (Matthew 10:16). Technology is a mixed bag. There is a lot to be concerned about but also a great deal to engage in and enjoy. Get out there in the tech world we live in; be open, but be on alert.

Tech Options *for* Younger Children

When you're exploring technology options for younger children, look for games and toys and gadgets that have the following characteristics:

- **ARE "ACTIVE, HANDS-ON, ENGAGING, AND EMPOWERING"**[26]

  The National Association for the Education of Young Children and the Fred Rogers Center recommend choosing technology and media that can be integrated into other activities. For example, you might take a trip to a museum and download their interactive app as you walk through the exhibits. Especially for younger children, these activities should be done with parents or other adults who can help guide the experience while still allowing the children to have some control.

■ "ENHANCE CHILDREN'S COGNITIVE AND SOCIAL ABILITIES"[27]

We still have access to manipulatives like blocks, art, books, pencils or crayons, and paper—and those should still be used. However, don't be afraid to add instructional or educational programs that allow children (over two years of age) to experience animals, objects, places, or people normally unavailable to them. There's a whole world out there to be explored. Your children need not miss out because of geographic location.

■ ARE "PLAYFUL AND SUPPORT CREATIVITY, EXPLORATION, PRETEND PLAY, ACTIVE PLAY, AND OUTDOOR ACTIVITIES"[28]

Not everything needs to be dry to be educational. Technology can and should be fun, and part of the fun is learning what you did wrong and how to make it right. Choose games and programs that allow for "self-correcting learning activities."[29]

■ "CAN HELP EDUCATORS MAKE AND STRENGTHEN HOME-SCHOOL CONNECTIONS"[30]

Schools are increasingly turning to technology to present and augment instruction. Teachers are also using technology to remain connected to students and their families.

DO YOUR HOMEWORK BEFORE YOU RUN OUT AND BUY THE LATEST GAME OR TOY OR GADGET.

All of these suggestions put you in control of the technology and the media you bring into the home. Do your homework before you run out and buy the latest game or toy or gadget. Read up on the product over the Internet. Ask other parents. Ask other kids. Be involved in how your children use what you've provided. Stay involved and active. Technology is a powerful tool that requires parental monitoring.

Tech Options *for* Teens

Exploring technology options for teens is much different from exploring the options for younger children, because teens are already using technology—and using it extensively.

The next two charts show percentages of teens with cell phones and smart phones.

"Almost all teenagers in America today have used social media." Those are startling statistics. No wonder they call this generation digital natives.

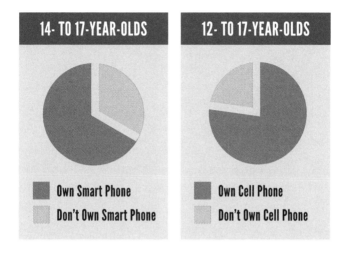

Teenagers are already using technology, if not in your home than in the home of friends or at school. If you've held off buying any tech and you wonder what technology teens today routinely interact with, *Consumer Reports* provides the top five tech gifts for teens, here given in reverse order:

5. *MP3 player*—This gadget has moved from just playing music to storing videos and podcasts.

4. *Tablet computer*—Since so much of what kids do is online, this gadget is a portable and cheap portal to the Internet.

3. *Laptop*—Many schools are encouraging the use of laptops for assignments, and some schools are even providing students with a laptop.

2. *Smartphone*—Because these phones can use bundles of data, be sure to set up a way to monitor your teen's use or you could be surprised by the monthly bill.

1. *Video game console*—These game consoles can be fun and instructive, especially when they're used to play with others.[33]

Teenagers are natural explorers. They are exploring themselves, their peers, their environment, their passions, and their interests. Technology gives them tools to expand their world. I suppose I see teens and the use of technology a bit like teens and the use of a vehicle. Eventually, most teenagers learn how to drive. As parents, we give them instructions in how to drive the car (or pay someone else to teach them in order to preserve our sanity) and then gradually increase our trust in them having control over such an expensive, powerful tool.

- We encourage teenagers to get a part-time job, so they can learn self-discipline and the skills needed to gain adult employment.

- We encourage teenagers to learn how to drive, so they can begin the process of becoming responsible to get from one place to another in one piece.

- We encourage teenagers to be involved in extracurricular activities, so they learn how to work within a group and gain valuable interpersonal skills.

- We insist teenagers go to school, so they learn how to learn and apply what they learn in academic and other settings.

Driving, jobs, sports, and school all put our teenagers in places outside of our influence. In each of those venues they will meet people and have experiences we can't control. At some point, each of us as parents must weigh the risks versus the rewards.

I have seen tremendous rewards with my kids where technology is concerned. I've been able to provide them with devices and programs that speak to their interests and passions. I am constantly astonished at the information they are able to access as they do their schoolwork and at the innovative ways educators are harnessing technology in the classroom. Our connection to technology has become a connection to each other, as we interact because of and through technology.

Technology is nothing more than a powerful tool. If we work with our children to learn how to handle the tool safely and effectively, their lives and ours will benefit. All things and situations in life are opportunities for us to share our hearts and our values.

> All things and situations in life are opportunities for us to share our hearts and our values.
>
> "TEACH THEM TO YOUR CHILDREN, TALKING ABOUT THEM WHEN YOU SIT AT HOME AND WHEN YOU WALK ALONG THE ROAD, WHEN YOU LIE DOWN AND WHEN YOU GET UP."
> —DEUTERONOMY 11:19

TIP #7

Look Inside, Not Just Outside

Megan was devastated. Her friend Rachel had tagged her in a terrible photo that never should have been posted in the first place. What was Rachel thinking? If Megan had taken that kind of picture of Rachel, she'd never have posted it anywhere and certainly wouldn't have tagged it.

Or was Rachel mad at her about something? Megan tried to think back over the party to see if there was anything that she had said or done to make Rachel mad at her. Was it a mistake? There was no way Rachel could think that was a good picture!

But if she de-tagged the photo, then Rachel would know she didn't like it. And Rachel still had the photo. If she was really mad at Megan for some reason, she could just text it or have someone else post it. Did

Megan really want to go around de-tagging the same photo multiple times? Talk about giving yourself away! Megan felt terrible. Now she could add worrying about Rachel to worrying about her looks.

■ ■ ■

The Heart *of the* Matter

Technology as a tool, I believe, acts like a mirror, revealing and magnifying what is already inside. If Megan hadn't already been worried about her looks, she wouldn't have cared about a random picture posted on Facebook. Because Megan was already hypersensitive, that picture had played directly into her fears about her attractiveness. If she hadn't already been unsure of her friendship with Rachel, she wouldn't have jumped to the conclusion that Rachel had posted the picture out of spite.

So many of the challenges presented by technology become a chicken-and-the-egg conundrum. For example, do girls concerned with their looks spend more time on media, or does media cause girls to worry more about their looks? One study determined that teen girls on Facebook were much more likely to be concerned with their body image—particularly their weight—than teen girls not on Facebook. However, "the direction of causality is unknown (it's possible that social network users differ from non-users in significant ways that make them particularly prone to media use, media messages, and societal pressures)."[34]

Another example: does being online create depression, or do depressed teenagers spend more time online? "People who spend a lot of time surfing the Internet are more likely to show signs of depression. . . . But it is not clear whether the Internet causes depression or whether depressed people are drawn to it."[35]

In my experience, parents—myself included—tend to look for outside factors to explain the concerns or behaviors of their children, instead of looking candidly at the children themselves. This tendency is so tempting. We

> Dangers from outside circumstances seem more distant and safer than dangers that might originate from inside the hearts of our children.
>
> "DON'T YOU SEE THAT WHATEVER ENTERS THE MOUTH GOES INTO THE STOMACH AND THEN OUT OF THE BODY? BUT THE THINGS THAT COME OUT OF A PERSON'S MOUTH COME FROM THE HEART, AND THESE DEFILE THEM."
> —MATTHEW 15:17–18

desperately hope that if we can just change the outside circumstances, then we can change our kids. Dangers from outside circumstances seem more distant and safer than dangers that might originate from inside the hearts of our children.

As parents, we must resist this tendency. We must not only watch what our children are doing with technology, but we must also seek to understand *why* they do what they do. Does the "outside," the technology, matter? Yes. But what matters more is the "inside," the heart.

Parents have fallen into the trap of looking for outside influences long before technology showed up. Parents have made excuses for poor grades by blaming teachers. They have explained away obesity by claiming bone structure. They have rationalized drug or alcohol addictions by pointing fingers at poor companions. As a therapist, I have seen and heard just about every excuse used by parents to deflect from the difficult truth that the problem was centered in the heart of their child.

Why do I bring this up in regard to technology? Because I want you to realize that children and teens may reveal part of their inner natures through their use of technology. Do you remember the story of Cindy and Tyler related at the beginning of "Tip #5: Watch Out for the Bad?" Without having learned about what had happened to Tyler, Cindy would not have known that he was quite socially awkward around his peers or that he was coming into his own sexual awareness. Teens are notoriously close-lipped about these coming-of-age challenges.

The How *and* Why *of the* Matter

As a parent, you have control over the *what* and the *when*—*what* the technology is that you bring into the house and *when* that technology can be used. Your children have control over the *how* and the *why*—*how* and *why* they will interact with that technology.

You may bring a game console into your house, but your son will reveal who he is through how and why he plays the games. He may play for sheer enjoyment with friends in real time or friends online, reveling in the spatial coordination, the competition, or bragging rights of the game. Or he may play for domination, single-mindedly choosing violent games to match his angry, aggressive nature. Same outside technology—different inside reasons.

You may give your daughter a smartphone, but she will reveal who she is by *why* she calls whom she does and by *how* she accesses the Internet with it. She may spend a lot of time chatting and texting with friends as a way to enhance her relationships. Or she may use Facebook or other social media as a way to establish queen-bee status over a group of peers. Same outside technology—different inside reasons.

> **Technology can reveal truths about the hearts of our children.**
>
> **"ABOVE ALL ELSE, GUARD YOUR HEART, FOR EVERYTHING YOU DO FLOWS FROM IT."**
> **—PROVERBS 4:23**

Please don't misunderstand me here: I'm not suggesting that all children or teens are wolves in sheep's clothing. What I am saying is that parents need to be alert to all aspects of their children's lives to monitor how those children are doing socially and emotionally, and one of the ways to monitor their children is through their use of technology. Watch for any warning signs that arise out of the use of technology, so you can investigate further and take action when needed.

Technology, as important as it is to children, can reveal truths about their hearts. Those hearts are precious—precious to you and precious to God.

TIP #8

Find Out What You Don't Know

"**Where** is Andy? Did you call his phone?" Brad was torn between frustration and concern, so he settled for both.

"Of course, I did," Brad's wife, Janice, answered. "Just went to voice mail."

"Why'd we get him the phone in the first place, if he won't answer it?" Janice, recognizing this as a rhetorical question, didn't answer. "What time was he supposed to be home?" Brad asked for the third time, a fact Janice chose to overlook.

She replied, "Ten."

"Have you called Justin's parents to see if they've heard from him?" That was one of the first things Janice had thought to do when Andy didn't answer the phone. But she hesitated, afraid that would alarm the Warners.

"No, let's give him another fifteen minutes to call back. If he hasn't called, we'll call again; and if he doesn't pick up, then we'll call the Warners."

■ ■ ■

Keeping Track

What parent of a teenager hasn't experienced something like this? Your kid isn't where he or she is supposed to be. You don't know what he or she is doing. You don't know if anything's wrong. Technology was supposed to create all these connections and provide all this information, but it's almost ten thirty at night and you still don't know what's going on.

In some ways, I need to watch that I'm not more complacent about where my oldest son is because he's got a cell phone. Growing up, I received a veritable inquisition whenever I wanted permission to leave the house, especially at night. "Where are you going?" "Who are you going with?" "What are you going to be doing?" "Are any adults going to be there?" "When will you be home?" If I didn't answer fully and correctly, the answer would be no. I wish I could say that I was always totally honest with my parents, but being a teenager, I sometimes downplayed certain aspects of my activities to gain permission. With technology, you have tools to gain answers when your kids won't give them.

Some parents may experience discomfort at the thought of spying on their kids. It's not spying if it's your kids. You are the parent and have responsibility over and for them. Why should kids be the only ones to take advantage of technology?

- Check out the phone and carrier your kids use for ways to monitor locations and activities. Any cell phone or smartphone can be located because it's constantly communicating with the "mother ship" (Verizon, Sprint, AT&T, T-Mobile, etc.). Large carriers have a service that allows parents to track their children's whereabouts based on the location of their phones. You can set automatic alerts that will let you know where your children are at a certain time of day. You can view historical data to find out where your children have been over the past several days. This works best when the cell phone is equipped with GPS. Otherwise, the location can only be narrowed down to the nearest cell phone tower, and that could be a radius of several miles.

- Check with your mobile carrier about a monitoring program that tracks the usage of your children's cell phones or smartphones. If your carrier doesn't offer the tracking or range of features you want, check out the monitoring programs recommended by Dr. Phil. He lists applications both for cell phones and for computers.[36]

- Use safety features on each tech device.

  - If you've got a PC running Windows, you can create a separate account for your children and utilize the Family Safety Settings. Through weekly reports, you can monitor what they're viewing and how long they're online. You can block content or even applications you don't want downloaded.

  - If you're a Mac household, you can turn on the Parental Control to do the same sort of monitoring. If you're not sure how to do this, my suggestion is not to ask your children. Instead, call the helpful tech person at your local Apple Store.

  - If your children have tablets, these same types of controls are available. Again, when in doubt, contact the manufacturer or the store where you purchased the items.

Still squeamish about these types of monitoring systems? Worried that you're turning into Big Brother? The more you know about what your children are really doing on all those devices, the better. Either you'll have confirmation that the rules and limits you've put in place are being respected, or you'll have factual data when you need to confront your children over unacceptable behavior.

> Spying is not a bad thing when you use it to protect your child. Children need protecting.
>
> "BE ALERT AND OF SOBER MIND. YOUR ENEMY THE DEVIL PROWLS AROUND LIKE A ROARING LION LOOKING FOR SOMEONE TO DEVOUR."
> —1 PETER 5:8

Maintaining Protection

There is another aspect to monitoring that I'd like you to consider. What if one of your children really needs help and is afraid to ask? What if one of your children has gotten in over his or her head and doesn't know how to back out? Maybe one of your children has inadvertently connected with the wrong person online or has received unwanted texts or messages from another person. Without monitoring your children's use of technology, you have no way of knowing if they need help straightening out an out-of-control situation.

Monitoring isn't spying, it's protecting. When you leave your house, you lock your door, right? When you park your car, don't you lock it? Why do you do those things? You do them because they are valuable things and have valuable things inside that you want to protect. Why wouldn't you want to "lock down" your child's technology and protect what's valuable on the outside and on the inside? Spying is not a bad thing when you use it to protect your child. Children need protecting.

Pray for the Best,
but Plan for the Worst

Brad could barely contain himself, waiting for Janice to get off the phone with the Warners. "Well, what did they say?"

Janice looked up, concern written all over her face. "Justin's been home for at least half an hour. Apparently, he and Andy were together earlier in the evening, but Andy took off with another boy after the game."

"Did he know who it was?" Brad felt like the floor had just dropped out from under him.

"No, just someone they met at the game. Justin said they kind of separated at the half, and he really didn't keep track after that."

"I thought Justin was supposed to bring Andy home after the game!" Brad gestured wildly in his agitation.

"That's what Andy told me," Janice admitted, "but that's not what Justin said. They were just supposed to meet at the game. Andy stayed late after school to help out some way—I don't really remember. He said Justin could take him home after the game."

"What do we do now?" Brad asked, just as Janice's cell phone rang.

Looking at the number, she blurted out to Brad, "It's Andy!" and quickly answered the phone. "Where are you?" she demanded.

After listening for just a moment, Janice interrupted and said, "Wait a minute. I'm going to put you on speaker, so Dad can hear."

Together, they listened to Andy explain how the game had gotten over early, so he'd gone with another kid from school who was going to grab something to eat. Somewhere along the way, the plans changed to go with some other boys and meet up with some girls in the next town. That's when Andy had backed out and said he wanted to go home. The other boys just mocked him and said they weren't turning around, and he could just get a ride home when they let him out. Janice's call had come while Andy was still in the car, and he hadn't wanted to answer in front of the other boys. Now he was stuck at eleven thirty at night outside of a 7-11 and could someone please come and pick him up?

"I'll go," Brad said without any hesitation. Janice could hear Andy's hesitation on the other end.

"Okay, Dad, here's the address. I'll be waiting for you."

■ ■ ■

Best Laid Plans

The plan for the cell phone was for Andy to use it to communicate with his parents. That didn't happen. So what do you do when the rules and the limits on technology aren't followed? What do you do if your son goes onto a porn site? What do you do if your daughter gives out personal information to someone she's met online? What do you do if your son or your daughter posts an angry rant—about you—on social media?

I pray that doesn't happen to you, but I've sat in my office with too many parents explaining how all of the boundaries and rules and limits they had set around their children hadn't held and something bad had happened. Crises with children aren't new to technology. There are, however, a few simple steps you can take in the midst of a crisis—technology related or not—to help create solutions.

■ STAY CALM

You may feel like lashing out or tearing your hair out, but that's not going to help the situation. A frightened, defiant, or humiliated child does not need a yelling, crying, vengeful parent. It may not be easy to stay calm, but you're the adult and you need to act like one.

■ CREATE DIALOGUE

As a parent, you may want to launch into a soliloquy on how stupid and reckless and disrespectful your child is, but I urge you not to do so. In the midst of a crisis, you need to gain your child's trust, so you can get at the truth of the situation. Your child can't communicate with you if you're doing all the talking.

■ FOCUS ON WHAT'S MOST IMPORTANT

In Andy's case, what was most important was getting him safely home. That was the first order of business. The details of how he got into that mess in the first place and any repercussions that would result from his misbehavior could wait. Take care of first things first and generally, in a crisis, the first thing is safety.

■ CREATE SPACE

Once the most important things are taken care of, you can give your child time to process with you what has happened and why. This type of evaluation is best done away from the fire of the crisis. Let your child know you need to work through the situation further, and let him or her know when that time will be.

Of course, if your child is ready to talk about it, go right ahead! Just realize you may also need some time to decide how best to deal with what you're hearing. You don't need to deliver an immediate answer, but you do need to let your child know that you will provide one.

■ COLLABORATE ON CONSEQUENCES

If you've already set consequences in place for breaking rules, then those consequences should be implemented. Whenever possible, bring your child into the discussion of consequences. You may find that out of shame and guilt for their behavior, they are harder on themselves than you would be.

■ DON'T MISS A TEACHABLE MOMENT

God promises to make all things work together for good (Romans 8:28). "All things" encompasses a great deal, so don't doubt that God can take this crisis and turn it around to produce something valuable and worthwhile. Helping your child look for and reach for the positives will help him or her redeem the experience.

> Helping your child look for and reach for the positives will help him or her redeem the experience.
>
> "CONSIDER IT PURE JOY, MY BROTHERS AND SISTERS, WHENEVER YOU FACE TRIALS OF MANY KINDS, BECAUSE YOU KNOW THAT THE TESTING OF YOUR FAITH PRODUCES PERSEVERANCE."
> —JAMES 1:2–3

■ PRAY

There will be a time for you to break down and feel the full brunt of the stress of the crisis. When this happens, ask God for wisdom, strength, and endurance.

Keep Up with Changes

"*Why* should I get a new iPhone? The one I have works perfectly well." Paula knew Hannah didn't bring this up because she was concerned about Paula getting a new iPhone. This was all about *Hannah* getting a new iPhone, since they were on the same plan. Hannah, rapid fire, started listing off a series of benefits. Paula felt she needed an interpreter. Nothing Hannah said made any sense, except, maybe, the rose-gold color option.

"How much is it?" Paula asked, inwardly wincing.

"Four hundred dollars, but you can get it for less when you sign up for a plan," Hannah said confidently.

"So this is the 6S?" Paula asked, just wanting to make sure she understood.

"Yes." Hannah seemed pleased that her mother was keeping up.

"Well, when does the 7S come out?" Paula wanted to know.

"Not for another year!" Hannah wailed, fearful Paula was going to bypass the 6S altogether for the 7S.

Paula wondered to herself, *When will this end?* The only answer she could come up with was when Hannah was old enough to buy her own phone.

■ ■ ■

Exponential Technology

Since 1965, the tech world has been operating under something known as Moore's Law, which states that computing power doubles every 18 to 24 months. For a while, there was doubt Moore's Law would make it through the end of the year, but IBM apparently has found a way to keep it alive by producing computing "circuits [that are] 10,000 times thinner than human hairs." [37] Moore's Law speaks to the historical reality that computers are becoming smaller and faster and have greater memory capacity.

Computers now design computers and other technology. This is called exponential technology. The cumulative effect of technology appears to be greater than the sum of its parts. There are some who claim that the new supercomputers are gaining fast on the human brain, which is now said to be only thirty times faster than a supercomputer.[38]

In 1975, Bill Gates and Paul Allen started Microsoft. In 1976, Steve Jobs and Steve Wozniak started Apple. Consider what has happened since then:

- We have gone from a world without personal computers to a world with computers so personal we keep them in our back pockets.

- We have gone from writing letters and placing calls on handsets to texts and tweets on cell phones.

- We have gone from expecting results in days or weeks to expecting results in seconds or minutes.

The world has changed and so have our kids. Our children are the first generation in this brave new world.

The first generation of Japanese born in the United States are known as *Nisei*.[39] I read a fascinating comparison of first generation Japanese to first generation netizens—citizens of the Net (Internet). The idea is that our kids are the first generation to be born into a digital world. They've never known existence without technology on hand at all times. Consequently, they never had to adjust themselves to it the way those of us in older generations have. They understand this new world in an intuitive, natural way the rest of us can't. "The drumbeat of disruption and technological advance that has defined the past 20 years is their natural rhythm."[40]

THE WORLD HAS CHANGED AND SO HAVE OUR KIDS. OUR CHILDREN ARE THE FIRST GENERATION IN THIS BRAVE NEW WORLD.

Lifelong Learners

My final parenting tip is one I anticipate with both excitement and dread. Part of me wants the pace of this technology to slow down—at least long enough for my brain to outlast a supercomputer—but slowing doesn't appear to be happening this year, anyway. As parents, we cannot rest on our laurels (or anywhere else, for that matter) where technology is concerned. We simply need to resign ourselves to staying lifelong learners in the technology category, even when the pace of change is not our natural rhythm. After our kids grow up and move out (hopefully), the day will come when we'll need to interact with our grandchildren over whatever is the latest and greatest.

ALLOWING YOUR CHILD TO BE IN A POSITION OF KNOWLEDGE DOES NOT MEAN YOU ABDICATE AUTHORITY.

- ## KEEP UP WITH TECHNOLOGY IN THE NEWS.

  You don't have to own a device to understand what it is and what it does. If your child was interested in auto mechanics or the Pittsburgh

Steelers or 12-string guitars, wouldn't you at least make yourself aware of these things, so you could have an intelligent, informed conversation?

■ LET YOUR CHILD TEACH YOU ABOUT THE TECHNOLOGY.

As a parent, it's not your job to know everything. You can't, so it's a useless endeavor. There is nothing demeaning about asking your child to explain devices or technology that you don't understand. Allowing your child to be in a position of knowledge does not mean you abdicate authority.

■ WHENEVER IT MAKES SENSE, PURCHASE NEW TECHNOLOGY.

Granted, purchasing new technology can be an expensive endeavor, but some technology isn't that pricey. Try to find a middle ground between hanging on to your ten-year-old laptop and rushing out to get the latest game fifteen minutes after it's released.

■ ASK OTHER PARENTS ABOUT THE TECHNOLOGY THEY HAVE AND USE.

Utilize the wisdom of the crowd with other parents, and spread your knowledge around.

The good news in all of this is that God's wisdom is available and applicable, no matter what the future holds. The future changes, but God never does.

> "EVERY GOOD AND PERFECT GIFT IS FROM ABOVE, COMING DOWN FROM THE FATHER OF THE HEAVENLY LIGHTS, WHO DOES NOT CHANGE LIKE SHIFTING SHADOWS." —JAMES 1:17

The future changes, but human nature tends to remain fairly consistent.

> "WHAT HAS BEEN WILL BE AGAIN, WHAT HAS BEEN DONE WILL BE DONE AGAIN; THERE IS NOTHING NEW UNDER THE SUN." —ECCLESIASTES 1:9

God is fully prepared to give you what you need whenever you need it to deal with whatever technology the future holds.

> "GOD IS ABLE TO BLESS YOU ABUNDANTLY, SO THAT IN ALL THINGS AT ALL TIMES, HAVING ALL THAT YOU NEED, YOU WILL ABOUND IN EVERY GOOD WORK."—2 CORINTHIANS 9:8

Don't fear—parenting is *very* good work.

Notes

2. "Parents, Privacy and Technology Use," (Full Report), *Family Online Safety Institute* (November 17, 2015): 1, https://www.fosi.org/policy-research/parents-privacy-technology-use (accessed November 19, 2015).

3. "88% of Parents Concerned About What Children Can Access Online, Reveals Survey," *ESET* (August 20, 2015), http://www.eset.com/int/about/press/articles/products/article/88-of-parents-concerned-about-what-children-can-access-online-reveals-survey (accessed November 19, 2015).

4. Barna Group, "The Family and Technology Report," *State of the Church and Family* (2011 Annual Report): 8.

5. Fisher-Price, "Fisher-Price Ipad Apptivity Seat, Newborn-to-Toddler," *Amazon*, http://www.amazon.com/Fisher-Price-Apptivity-Newborn--Discontinued-Manufacturer/dp/B00EL4NI5U/ref=sr_1_3?ie=UTF8&qid=1447980962&sr=8-3&keywords=iPad+Activity+seat (accessed November 19, 2015).

6. PassivelySedentary, "Human Dystopia," *YouTube* (August 30, 2011), https://www.youtube.com/watch?v=h1BQPV-iCkU.

7. "Managing Media: We Need a Plan," *American Association of Pediatrics* (October 28, 2013), https://www.aap.org/en-us/about-the-aap/aap-press-room/pages/managing-media-we-need-a-plan.aspx (accessed January 14, 2016).

8. Tara Haelle, "Most Preschoolers Use Tablets, Smartphones Daily," *WebMD News from HealthDay* (November 2, 2015), http://www.webmd.com/parenting/news/20151102/most-

preschoolers-use-tablets-smartphones-daily (accessed November 19, 2015).

9. Ibid.

10. "Media and Children," *American Academy of Pediatrics*, https:// www.aap.org/en-us/advocacy-and-policy/aap-health-initiatives/ pages/media-and-children.aspx (accessed November 25, 2015).

11. McCann World Group, "Today's Global Youth Would Give Up Their Sense of Smell to Keep Their Technology: Study Examines the First Really Global Generation," *PR Newswire* (May 25, 2011), http://www.prnewswire.com/news-releases/ todays-global-youth-would-give-up-their-sense-of-smell-to-keep-their-technology-122605643.html (accessed November 25, 2015).

12. "Teens and Sleep," *National Sleep Foundation*, https:// sleepfoundation.org/sleep-topics/teens-and-sleep (accessed December 2, 2015).

13. Amanda L. Gamble, et al., "Adolescent Sleep Patterns and Night-Time Technology Use," *PLOS One* (November 12, 2014), http://journals.plos.org/plosone/article?id=10.1371/journal. pone.0111700 (accessed December 2, 2015).

14. "Teens and Sleep," *National Sleep Foundation*.

15. Matt Sloane, "'Text Neck' and Other Tech Troubles," *WebMD News* (November 26, 2014): 1, http://www.webmd.com/pain-management/news/20141124/text-neck (accessed December 2, 2015).

16. Chris Adams, "What Is Texting Thumb?" *About.com* (December 15, 2014), http://ergonomics.about.com/od/De-Quervains_ Syndrome/a/What_Is_Texting_Thumb.htm (accessed December 2, 2015).

17. Linda Stone, "Continuous Partial Attention," *The Attention Project* (March 11, 2015), http://lindastone.net/qa/continuous-partial-attention (accessed December 3, 2015).

18. Ibid.

19. Maura Nevel Thomas, *Personal Productivity Secrets* (Indianapolis, IN: Wiley and Sons, Inc., 2012): 11.

20. "APA Review Confirms Link Between Playing Violent Video Games and Aggression," *American Psychological Association* (August 13, 2015), http://www.apa.org/news/press/releases/2015/08/violent-video-games.aspx (accessed November 25, 2015).

21. Benny Evangelista, "Attention Loss Feared as HighTech Rewires Brain," *SFGate* (November 15, 2009), http://www.sfgate.com/business/article/Attention-loss-feared-as-high-tech-rewires-brain-3281030.php (accessed December 3, 2015).

22. Nicholas Carr, *The Shallows: What the Internet Is Doing to Our Brains* (NY: W. W. Norton and Company, Inc., 2010).

23. Victoria Rideout, "Social Media, Social Life: How Teens View Their Digital Lives," *Common Sense* (June 26, 2012): 25, https://www.commonsensemedia.org/research/social-media-social-life-how-teens-view-their-digital-lives (accessed December 3, 2015).

24. Ibid.

25. "Luddite" is a slang term for someone who opposes new technology. If you want to read more about the etymology of the term, go to http://www.history.com/news/ask-history/who-were-the-luddites.

26. The National Association for the Education of Young Children and the Fred Rogers Center for Early Learning and Children's

Media at Saint Vincent College, "Technology and Interactive Media as Tools in Early Childhood Programs Serving Children from Birth through Age 8," *NAEYC* (January 2012): 5, http://www.naeyc.org/files/naeyc/file/positions/PS_technology_WEB2.pdf (accessed December 3, 2015).

27. Ibid., 6.

28. Ibid., 7.

29. Ibid.

30. Ibid.

31. Ibid.

32. Amanda Lenhart, "Teens, Smartphones and Texting," *Pew Research Center* (March 19, 2012): 3, http://www.pewinternet.org/files/old-media/Files/Reports/2012/PIP_Teens_Smartphones_and_Texting.pdf (accessed December 3, 2015).

33. Rideout, "Social Media, Social Life: How Teens View Their Digital Lives."

34. Kaitlyn Wells, "Top 5 Tech Gifts for Teenagers," *Consumer Reports* (December 18, 2013), http://www.consumerreports.org/cro/news/2013/12/top-5-tech-gifts-for-teenagers/index.htm (accessed December 3, 2015).

35. Seeta Pai and Kelly Schryver, "Children, Teens, Media and Body Image," *Common Sense* (January 21, 2015): 7, https://www.commonsensemedia.org/research/children-teens-media-and-body-image (accessed December 3, 2015).

36. Kate Kelland, "Study Links Excessive Internet Use to Depression," *Reuters*, ed. Paul Casciato (February 3, 2010), http://www.reuters.com/article/2010/02/03/us-depression-internet-idUSTRE61200A20100203#XGavq1Dk897G0 ZT7.97 (accessed December 3, 2015).

37. Phil McGraw, "How to Monitor Your Child's Cell Phone and Internet Activity," *Dr. Phil*, http://www.drphil.com/articles/article/603 (accessed December 3, 2015).

38. "Moore's Law Wins," *The Guardian* (July 9, 2015), http://www.theguardian.com/technology/2015/jul/09/moores-law-new-chips-ibm-7nm (accessed December 3, 2015).

39. Christian de Looper, "Research Suggests Human Brain Is 30 Times As Powerful As the Best Supercomputers, *Tech Times* (August 26, 2015), http://www.techtimes.com/articles/79701/20150826/research-suggusts-human-brain-30-times-powerful-best-supercomputers.htm (accessed December 3, 2015).

40. *Merriam-Webster,* s. v. "nisei," http://www.merriam-webster.com/dictionary/nisei (accessed February 1, 2016).

41. Jerry Adler, "Meet the First Digital Generation. Now Get Ready to Play by Their Rules," *Wired* (April 16, 2013), http://www.wired.com/2013/04/genwired (accessed December 3, 2015).